SPUDS

S·P·U·D·S

BRENDA BELL

CONTEMPORARY
BOOKS, INC.
CHICAGO

Library of Congress Cataloging in Publication Data

Bell, Brenda.
   Spuds : 50 great stuffed potato recipes.

   Includes index.
   1. Cookery (Potatoes)   I. Title.
TX803.P8B37   1985   636.6′521   85-14959
ISBN 0-8092-5161-2

Published by Contemporary Books, Inc.
180 North Michigan Avenue, Chicago, Illinois 60601
Manufactured in the United States of America
Library of Congress Catalog Card Number: 85-14959
International Standard Book Number: 0-8092-5161-2

Published simultaneously in Canada by Beaverbooks, Ltd.
195 Allstate Parkway, Valleywood Business Park
Markham, Ontario L3R 4T8 Canada

Heartfelt thanks to Bill for his encouragement, inspiration, and enthusiasm—and for serving as Number One taster and critic.

CONTENTS

INTRODUCTION

INTRODUCTION

It's true—the baked potato slathered with butter, salt, pepper, and sour cream is traditional, and to some, the way to a perfect baked potato. But, move over, traditionalists. The day of the modern stuffed potato has arrived!

The humble potato has climbed to new heights, finding its way into almost every meal occasion, from the elegant cocktail party to the everyday family dinner.

Trays of tiny new potatoes stuffed with the ultimate—sour cream and caviar—are the hottest thing in chic hors d'oeuvres. Fast food restaurants across the country boast potatoes with a choice of stuffings. There are even restaurants specializing in baked potatoes and glorious ways to stuff them.

And now, home cooks are enjoying the new-found pleasures of the meal-in-a-potato. Besides being a great choice nutritionally, potatoes are economical and available year-round. But most importantly, the potato might just be the most versatile food in the kitchen pantry.

It can be scooped, stuffed, and topped to make exciting main dishes with only a little imagination and a few ingredients. A quick glance into your cupboard or refrigerator right now will probably yield several palate-pleasing stuffing possibilities.

Read through the recipes here—they will serve as a guide to spur your imagination. You will soon begin to think of your favorite foods and recipes and how they will adapt as potato stuffers. Supermarkets, too, are brimming with convenience and prepared foods that make great stuffers.

Stuffed potatoes can star in almost any meal situation, too. From breakfast to late-night suppers, there's a perfect potato. Throughout these chapters are recipes and suggestions for

---

"A little dish oft furnishes enough, And sure enough is equal to a feast."

FIELDING
Covent Garden Tragedy

S·P·U·D·S

just about any meal occasion, from quick family dinners on the run to party-perfect potatoes.

And, speaking of party-perfect, a potato buffet is a fun and easy—not to mention delicious—way to entertain a few friends or a crowd. Offer a variety of stuffings and let guests help themselves to any combination they like. By serving a selection that includes cool, room-temperature, and hot stuffings, you will have a variety that should appeal to everyone—and it's much simpler to maintain than when everything must be served hot.

For another fun way to entertain, try a bring-a-stuffer supper, the newest relative of the traditional potluck dinner. Provide baked potatoes and the basics, such as plain and seasoned butter, sour cream, and cheeses, and have guests bring their specialties.

The beauty of it is, of course, that almost anything goes when it's potato-stuffing time. Chili, stews, soups, stir-fries, vegetables, cheese spreads, creamy dips, and more make perfect stuffers.

NUTRITIVE VALUE— NOT TO BE OVERLOOKED

The potato is a great meal choice, especially now, in light of current nutritional recommendations to increase consumption of complex carbohydrates, including fruits and vegetables. The reason? Complex carbohydrates are major energy sources for the body, providing such important nutrients as vitamins, minerals, and fiber.

Consider these potato facts. A medium-size potato (about $\frac{1}{3}$ pound):

- provides about 110 calories,
- contributes important nutrients, including vitamin C, vitamin B_6, potassium, and fiber, to the diet,
- contains no cholesterol and no fat and is low in sodium.

Because it is believed that many potato nutrients are concentrated near the skin, it's a good idea to eat the skin as well as the interior of the potato.

4

INTRODUCTION

Of course, how you choose to stuff a potato plays a major role in the total calorie and nutrient content. Consider how the potato will be positioned within the day's meal plan—as a main dish or an accompaniment, as the major meal of the day or a light late-night snack.

The great thing about stuffing a potato, though, is the variety of stuffers to choose from—and the fact that you can control how much of the stuffer to use for each potato.

THE STUFFED POTATO PRIMER: THE WAY TO A PERFECT BAKED POTATO

Which Potato?

As you will undoubtedly notice on a trip through the produce aisles of your local grocery store, potato choices are not limited to just one or two. From the tiny red new potatoes, usually available March through August, to the familiar oblong russets, potato selections are plentiful all year long.

Although almost any potato can be baked, obviously some types are more acceptable than others. By all means, choose whatever type of potato you like and is most satisfactory.

A popular and widely available choice for baking are the russets, often called *baking potatoes*. These oblong potatoes have rough, thick skins and, after baking, a mealy, fluffy interior.

Selection

Choosing the perfect potato is the next step on the road to the ultimate stuffed potato. Adhering to a few basic selection principles will greatly enhance the outcome of the recipe.

Look for:

- clean, firm, smooth potatoes, free from blemishes and sprouts;
- regular shapes and sizes (important for even cooking) so that several potatoes finish baking at the same time.

Avoid:

- wrinkled, wilted skins; soft, dark areas; and cut surfaces;

5

- musty or moldy odors, which can give an off-flavor to the cooked potato;
- large green areas, which might give potatoes a bitter taste. Small areas of green can be cut away before eating.

Storage

For maximum eating enjoyment, store potatoes, unwashed, in a dark, well-ventilated place; about 45°F is the optimum storage temperature. Do not refrigerate. The lower the storage temperature, the greater the increase in sugar content, which can lead to the development of a sweet flavor and may cause potatoes to darken during cooking. If you can't store potatoes under optimum conditions, buy only enough to last a few days.

COOKING THE POTATO

Follow these suggestions to assure a perfectly cooked potato.

- Scrub potatoes gently but thoroughly with a vegetable brush under cold running water to remove dirt.
- Dry potatoes. Remove any sprouts or small green areas.
- Pierce potatoes with a fork in several places to allow steam to escape and to prevent potatoes from bursting during cooking.

If desired, potato skins can be rubbed with oil, butter, or bacon fat before cooking. This will produce a flavorful, soft exterior in contrast to the traditional dry, crusty exterior.

For a little different twist to coating the potato before baking, try a flavored butter or oil. Add one or more of the following to vegetable oil or softened butter or margarine. (Choose a seasoning to complement the stuffing you plan to use.)

- Garlic or onion—salt or powder
- Seasoned salt
- Celery salt
- Cayenne

INTRODUCTION

- Paprika
- Freshly ground black pepper
- Herbs—dried or fresh
- Mustard—dry or prepared

To Oven-Bake Potatoes

Place prepared potatoes on oven rack positioned in center of oven. (If potato has been coated with oil, butter, or fat, place in shallow pan on oven rack.) Bake in 425°F oven about 55–60 minutes or until potatoes are soft and yield to touch (use a mitt or hot pad to protect hands when testing a hot potato) or until they are soft in the center when tested with a fork.

Avoid cooking potatoes wrapped in foil unless you want a steamed potato. If you must hold potatoes before serving, however, wrap them in foil to help retain heat. Hold no longer than 20 minutes for maximum flavor and texture appeal.

To Microwave Potatoes

Microwaving is a fast way to cook potatoes without heating up your kitchen. Arrange medium to medium-large potatoes on paper toweling in microwave oven. Leave at least one inch of space between potatoes. (If potatoes are irregularly shaped, place the thickest part toward the outside to ensure more even, thorough cooking.)

Remember that cooking time increases as the number of potatoes increases. Use the chart below as a *general guideline* for microwaving times.

Number of Potatoes	Cooking Time (HIGH—100% Power)
1	4–5 minutes
2	6–8 minutes
3	9–10 minutes
4	11–13 minutes
5	14–16 minutes
6	17–18 minutes

Numerous factors can affect the outcome of microwaving. Time is affected by the size, shape, and weight as well as the moisture content of each potato. Also, microwave ovens vary greatly from one brand to another, so your oven may require more or less cooking time than indicated in the table.

Note: Some microwave oven manufacturers suggest turning potatoes and rearranging halfway through the cooking time. It's always a good idea to check the instruction manual for your particular oven to get the best microwaving results.

STUFFING THE POTATO

Stuffed potato is a loosely concocted, all-inclusive term covering everything from the good old-fashioned "twice-baked" potato to simply fluffing the interior and topping with a flavored butter or sauce, allowing juices and flavorings to seep into the potato. Just remember that, whatever the stuffing method, the key is to use flavorful ingredients that taste delicious when piled into the perfectly baked potato.

Unless otherwise indicated, potatoes in these recipes should be prepared for stuffing as follows:

Just prior to serving, make a single cut or a cross-shaped cut in the top of each potato. Open potato by pressing ends and sides toward center to fluff the interior of the potato (use a mitt or hot pad to protect hands). You might wish to use a fork to fluff the interior even more, to allow sauces and seasonings to flavor the potato throughout. In some recipes, it is desirable to open the potato to form a sort of bowl, especially for stuffings that have lots of sauce.

If desired, after fluffing you may add salt, pepper, butter, or other seasonings to the potato, then spoon on the stuffing. It's purely a matter of personal preference, often influenced by the type of stuffing to be used.

All recipes are based on potatoes weighing *6–8 ounces.* The size of the potato can be varied, of course, depending on whether the

INTRODUCTION

potato is a main dish or an accompaniment and on whether the appetite is big or small.

If desired, half of a potato may be substituted for the whole potato. Simply cut the potato in half lengthwise, fluff interior, and continue as you would with a whole potato.

RECIPE TIPS

These recipes are meant as guides and inspirations. There's always room for changes according to personal taste preferences.

One area where this is particularly true is seasonings. Use more or less as taste indicates. Omit the salt; increase the herbs. Feel free to substitute favorite cheese varieties or to use margarine in place of butter. The recipes are flexible—they can stand a little modification if you so desire.

> *"The best and most wholesome feeding is upon one dish and no more and the same plain and simple. . . ."*
>
> **PLINY**
> ***Historia Naturalis***

DAIRY STUFFERS

DAIRY STUFFERS

If you thought butter, sour cream, and a sprinkling of cheese made the perfect baked potato, think again. While these do dress a potato in a most delicious way, they are only the beginning of the taste-tempting treats that stuff the modern baked potato.

Consider savory flavored butters, herbed cheeses, and sour cream combinations. Don't overlook tangy yogurt, creamy cottage cheese, and velvety-smooth cheese sauces—all of which decidedly complement the flavor of a baked potato. And there's more!

Eggs and potatoes have long been a favorite mealtime duo, but just wait until you've topped a baked potato with eggs. They're bound to become favorites. Potatoes Benedict—lemony Hollandaise and poached eggs are right at home atop a perfectly baked potato. Corned beef hash with potatoes might be a standard, but now there's a new twist. A tasty hash spooned into a potato, topped with a sunny-side-up egg, will delight all who taste it.

Versatile dairy stuffers take their place as both mealtime accompaniments and main dishes, starring in every meal, from breakfast to late-night supper. Enjoy!

> "Sit down and feed, and welcome to our table."
>
> **SHAKESPEARE**
> *As You Like It*

11

CLASSIC CHEESE SAUCE POTATOES

Served alone or with favorite vegetables or ham, cheese sauce and baked potatoes just naturally go together.

Makes 4 servings

2 tablespoons butter or margarine

2 tablespoons all-purpose flour

1 cup milk

Dash salt

Dash white pepper

1 cup shredded cheddar, American, or Swiss cheese

4 baked potatoes

In medium saucepan, melt butter over medium-low heat. Stir in flour until smooth. Slowly stir in milk, salt, and pepper. Cook and stir until thickened and smooth, increasing heat to medium if necessary. Remove from heat. Stir in cheese until melted. Spoon about ¼ cup sauce over each potato.

VARIATIONS:

Broccoli: Arrange cooked broccoli flowerets over each potato; spoon sauce over.

Vegetable: Add 1 cup favorite cooked vegetables to sauce; spoon over potato.

Tomato: Layer chopped tomato over each potato; spoon sauce over.

Ham: Add 1 cup cubed cooked ham to sauce; spoon over potato.

CANNELLONI-STYLE STUFFER

*This Italian-style potato is a meal in itself.
Make some ahead to keep in the freezer
for those days when time is short.*

Makes 4 servings

4 baked potatoes

1 cup ricotta cheese

2 tablespoons butter or margarine

1 egg, beaten

Dash salt

Milk

2 tablespoons chopped green onion

2 tablespoons chopped parsley

Grated Parmesan cheese

*Marinara Sauce (canned or homemade),
   heated*

Remove thin slice from top of each potato. Gently scoop out inside of each potato, leaving skin intact. Combine potato, ricotta, butter, egg, and salt. Beat until smooth and fluffy or to desired consistency. (Mixture should be fairly stiff.) Add milk if mixture seems too stiff. Stir in onion, parsley, and 2 tablespoons Parmesan cheese. Fill skins with potato mixture, mounding high. Sprinkle additional Parmesan over each potato if desired. Bake at 400°F for about 10 minutes or until heated through or cook in the microwave at HIGH (100%) power 3–5 minutes or until heated through. Serve with Marinara Sauce.

If desired, cooked potatoes may be wrapped securely and frozen until needed. To serve, unwrap and place in shallow pan. Heat at 350°F about 20–30 minutes until completely heated through. To microwave, unwrap and heat at high power about 5 minutes for one potato, or 7 minutes for two.

CREAMY CHIVE POTATOES

Traditional cream cheese flavored with chives will always be a favorite. Make these ahead and freeze until needed.

Makes 4 servings

4 baked potatoes

2 packages (3 ounces each) cream cheese, softened

2 tablespoons butter or margarine

Salt and pepper

Milk

2 tablespoons minced chives

Remove thin slice from top of each potato. Gently scoop out inside of each potato, leaving skin intact. Combine potato, cream cheese, and butter. Add salt and pepper to taste. Beat until smooth and fluffy or to desired consistency. (Mixture will be fairly stiff.) Add milk if mixture seems too stiff. Stir in chives. Fill skins with potato mixture, mounding high. Bake at 400°F for about 10 minutes or until heated through or cook in the microwave at **HIGH** (100%) power 3–5 minutes or until heated through.

If desired, cooked potatoes may be wrapped securely and frozen until needed. To serve, unwrap and place in shallow pan. Heat at 350°F about 20–30 minutes until completely heated through. To microwave, unwrap and heat at high power about 5 minutes for one potato, or 7 minutes for two.

DAIRY STUFFERS

STUFFED POTATOES OLE

These stuffed potatoes with a zip can be frozen and reheated.

Makes 4 servings

4 baked potatoes

2 tablespoons butter or margarine

Dairy sour cream

Salt

1¼ cups shredded Monterey Jack cheese with jalapeño peppers

¼ cup chopped pitted ripe olives

Remove thin slice from top of each potato. Gently scoop out inside of each potato, leaving skin intact. Combine potato, butter, ¾ cup sour cream, and salt to taste. Beat until smooth and fluffy or to desired consistency. (Mixture will be fairly stiff.) Add additional sour cream if mixture seems too stiff. Stir in cheese and olives. Fill skins with potato mixture, mounding high. Bake at 400°F for about 10 minutes or until heated through or cook in the microwave at HIGH (100%) power 3–5 minutes or until heated through.

If desired, cooked potatoes may be wrapped securely and frozen until needed. To serve, unwrap and place in shallow pan. Heat at 350°F about 20–30 minutes until completely heated through. To microwave, unwrap and heat at high power about 5 minutes for one potato, or 7 minutes for two.

CHEDDAR STUFFER

Cheddar cheese and potatoes are a natural, and this recipe allows you to savor the cheesy flavor throughout. Prepare ahead and freeze; add sprinkling of cheddar just before baking.

Makes 4 servings

4 baked potatoes

2 tablespoons butter or margarine

Dairy sour cream

Salt and pepper

1¼ cups shredded cheddar cheese

Remove thin slice from top of each potato. Gently scoop out inside of each potato, leaving skin intact. Combine potato, butter, and ¾ cup sour cream. Add salt and pepper to taste. Beat until smooth and fluffy or to desired consistency. (Mixture will be fairly stiff.) Add additional sour cream if mixture seems too stiff. Stir in 1 cup of the shredded cheddar cheese. Fill skins with potato mixture, mounding high. Sprinkle remaining ¼ cup shredded cheese evenly over each potato, if desired. Bake at 400°F for about 10 minutes or until heated through or cook in the microwave at **HIGH** (100%) power 3–5 minutes or until heated through.

If desired, cooked potatoes may be wrapped securely and frozen until needed. To serve, unwrap and place in shallow pan. Heat at 350°F about 20–30 minutes until completely heated through. To microwave, unwrap and heat at high power about 5 minutes for one potato, or 7 minutes for two.

VARIATION

Add 3 slices crisp-cooked, crumbled bacon and/or 2 tablespoons chopped green onion along with cheese.

ZESTY COTTAGE CHEESE POTATOES

Tangy cottage cheese is great for topping potatoes, but it's even more special when flavored with onion and horseradish.

Makes 6 servings

1 cup cream-style cottage cheese

¼ cup plain yogurt

2 teaspoons grated onion

1½ teaspoons prepared horseradish

½ teaspoon seasoned salt (optional)

6 baked potatoes

Chopped chives

Blend together cottage cheese, yogurt, onion, horseradish, and salt. Refrigerate at least 1 hour to allow flavors to blend. Top each potato with cottage cheese and chives.

EASY CHEESY SAUCE

A three-ingredient quick cheese sauce that couldn't be simpler to prepare!

Makes 4 servings

1 container (8 ounces) cold-pack cheese food sharp cheddar, Swiss, garlic, or other flavor)

½ cup dairy sour cream

2 tablespoons butter or margarine

4 baked potatoes

Beat cheese, sour cream, and butter on high speed of electric mixer until smooth. Spoon sauce over potato. (Sauce may be served heated if desired.)

Note: This sauce is excellent when served with Classic Cheese Sauce Potatoes variations (see Chapter 1).

HERBED CREAM CHEESE POTATOES

A creamy, savory topping you'll want to keep on hand; try with fresh herbs too.

Makes 4–6 servings

1 package (8 ounces) cream cheese, softened

1 cup shredded cheddar or Swiss cheese (optional)

1 tablespoon minced chives

1 teaspoon fines herbes, or a combination of your favorite fresh or dried herbs to taste

½ teaspoon freshly ground black pepper

4–6 baked potatoes

Beat cream cheese on high speed of electric mixer until light and fluffy. Stir in cheddar cheese, chives, herbes, and pepper. Chill at least 1 hour to allow flavors to blend. Allow to soften slightly before spooning over potatoes.

> *"Oh, better, no doubt,*
> *is a dinner of herbs,*
> *When season'd by love which*
> *no rancour disturbs. . . ."*
>
> **OWEN MEREDITH**
> *Lucile*

POTATOES BENEDICT

CORNED BEEF
AND EGG POTATOES

DILLED SALMON AND
CUCUMBER POTATOES

BASIL SHRIMP AND CHICKEN

POTATOES BENEDICT

Company-perfect for brunch, traditional Eggs Benedict teamed with baked potato—a rave-winning combination.

Makes 4 servings

8 thin slices fully cooked Canadian bacon or ham (warm)

4 baked potatoes

4 poached eggs

1 cup Hollandaise Sauce (see recipe below)

Sliced pitted ripe olives

Parsley sprigs

Place 2 slices bacon on each potato, pressing into potato. Place egg on top of bacon. Spoon Hollandaise Sauce over each egg. Garnish with olives and parsley if desired.

Quick Food Processor Hollandaise: Using metal blade in food processor, process 3 egg yolks, 2 tablespoons lemon juice, dash of salt, and dash of cayenne until thick and lemon-colored, about 3 seconds. With machine running, add ½ cup butter (melted to bubbling stage) in slow, steady stream. Makes about 1 cup. As an alternative, use your own favorite recipe or a packaged mix.

Yield: about 1 cup

VARIATION

Florentine Potatoes Benedict: Place 2–3 tablespoons warm, cooked chopped spinach, seasoned to taste, on top of bacon. With back of spoon, make indentation in spinach. Place egg on top of spinach. Continue as directed above.

COUNTRY BREAKFAST POTATOES

Scrambled eggs deluxe, and never better.

Makes 4 servings

2 tablespoons chopped green bell pepper (optional)

¼ cup chopped onion

1 tablespoon butter or margarine

½ cup diced cooked ham or ½ cup cooked, drained, and crumbled bulk pork sausage

4 eggs, beaten with 2 tablespoons water

Salt and pepper

4 baked potatoes

¼ cup shredded cheddar cheese (optional)

In medium skillet, cook green pepper and onion in butter over medium-low heat until tender. Stir in ham. Add eggs to skillet. Cook over medium-low heat until eggs begin to set on bottom and sides; lift and fold to allow uncooked portion to set. Continue cooking until eggs are soft-scrambled, or to desired doneness. Season to taste with salt and pepper. Spoon eggs over each potato. Sprinkle 1 tablespoon cheese over each.

VARIATION

Omit cheese. Spoon favorite cheese sauce over each potato.

CORNED BEEF AND EGG POTATOES

A new twist to a traditional dish—hash served inside a potato.

Makes 4 servings

½ cup chopped onion
¼ cup finely chopped green bell pepper
2 tablespoons butter or margarine
2 cups finely chopped cooked corned beef
Salt and pepper
4 baked potatoes
4 eggs, cooked sunny side up
2 tablespoons chopped chives

In medium skillet, cook onion and green pepper in butter over medium heat until tender. Stir in corned beef; heat through. Season to taste with salt and pepper. Divide hash mixture evenly among potatoes. Make indentation in hash with back of spoon. Place egg in indentation. Sprinkle with chives. Serve immediately.

> *"A good, honest, wholesome, hungry breakfast."*
>
> **WALTON**
> *The Compleat Angler*

BLUE CHEESE TOPPING

A deluxe blue cheese topping that's delicious alone or with a sprinkling of crumbled bacon.

Makes 4 servings

3 tablespoons crumbled blue cheese

1 cup (8 ounces) dairy sour cream

Dash salt

1 green onion, chopped fine

1 clove garlic, minced

½ teaspoon Worcestershire sauce

4 baked potatoes

Combine cheese, sour cream, salt, onion, garlic, and Worcestershire sauce. Stir to blend well. Refrigerate at least 1 hour to allow flavors to blend. Spoon about ¼ cup topping over each potato.

DILL-ICIOUS BUTTER

Dill and potatoes are long-standing favorites; keep this butter handy for dressing up any meal.

Makes ½ cup

½ cup butter or margarine, softened

1 tablespoon chopped fresh dill or 1 teaspoon dried dill weed

1 tablespoon finely chopped green onion

Dash salt (optional)

Baked potatoes

Beat butter until very light and fluffy. Stir in dill, onion, and salt. Cover; refrigerate at least 2 hours to allow flavors to blend. Spoon desired amount over each potato.

Note: This butter keeps well, refrigerated and covered, up to 2 weeks.

HERB BUTTER

GARDEN YOGURT TOPPER

Simple to prepare, Herb Butter quickly transforms plain baked potatoes into potatoes extraordinaire.

Makes ½ cup

½ cup butter or margarine, softened
1 clove garlic, minced
2 tablespoons chopped chives
2 tablespoons chopped parsley
⅛–¼ teaspoon freshly ground black pepper
Baked potatoes

Beat butter and garlic until very light and fluffy. Stir in chives, parsley, and pepper. Spoon desired amount over each potato.
Note: this butter keeps well, refrigerated and covered, up to 2 weeks.

Crunchy and crisp vegetables combined with tangy yogurt make a refreshing potato topper.

Makes 4 servings

1 cup plain yogurt
2 tablespoons chopped radish
2 tablespoons chopped green bell pepper
1 tablespoon chopped green onion
1 tablespoon chopped parsley
1 medium tomato, chopped
4 baked potatoes

Combine yogurt, radish, green pepper, green onion, and parsley. Refrigerate at least 1 hour to allow flavors to blend. Just before serving, stir in tomato. Spoon yogurt over each potato.

23

MEAT, POULTRY, AND SEAFOOD FAVORITES

Baked potatoes aren't just side dishes anymore! Now they can be the main attraction at any meal. Stuff a potato with everything from soup to stew to salads—even favorite sandwich fixings—and you won't be disappointed.

Potatoes are equally enticing stuffed with a rich, sour-cream-sauced stroganoff or a cool, tangy dill and yogurt salmon salad. You'll find that hot baked potatoes readily take on delicately flavored pan juices or hearty, robust gravies.

As you prepare main dish stuffings, you'll realize that many of your own favorite dishes will make excellent stuffers because almost "anything goes" into a stuffed baked potato.

> *"Let the stoics say what they please, we do not eat for the good of living, but because the meat is savory and the appetite is keen."*
>
> **EMERSON**
> *Essays, Second Series: Nature*

TANGY MEATBALL STUFFING

Potatoes stuffed with meatballs in a tangy tomato sauce are an unbeatable combination, destined to become a family favorite. Try them with a sprinkling of cheddar or Parmesan.

Makes 4 servings

1 pound ground beef
1 cup soft, fine bread crumbs
2 tablespoons chopped parsley
1 tablespoon instant minced onion
½ teaspoon seasoned salt
1 egg, beaten
1 tablespoon vegetable oil
1 can (8 ounces) tomato sauce
¾ cup water

½ cup coarsely chopped green bell pepper (optional)
⅓ cup chopped onion
2 tablespoons vinegar
2 tablespoons brown sugar
2 teaspoons prepared mustard
4 baked potatoes

Combine beef, crumbs, parsley, minced onion, salt, and egg. Stir to mix well. Shape into 1-inch meatballs. In large deep skillet, brown meatballs in oil over medium-low heat; turn frequently to brown on all sides. (Brown meatballs in several batches if necessary to avoid overcrowding skillet.) Remove meatballs; drain well. Drain excess fat from skillet. Add tomato sauce, water, green pepper, chopped onion, vinegar, sugar, and mustard to skillet; stir to combine. Return meatballs to skillet. Bring to a boil. Reduce heat and simmer, covered, 30 minutes, stirring occasionally. Spoon meatballs and sauce over each potato.

EASY STROGANOFF TOPPER

The tangy sour cream sauce and tender strips of beef are right at home atop a potato.

Makes 4 servings

½ *pound boneless sirloin steak, cut* ½ *inch thick*

3 tablespoons butter or margarine

½ *cup chopped onion*

2 cloves garlic, minced (optional)

1 cup sliced mushrooms

¼ *cup beef broth*

1 tablespoon tomato paste

1 cup (8 ounces) dairy sour cream

4 baked potatoes

Cut sirloin into strips about ¼ inch thick and 2 inches in length. In large skillet, cook sirloin strips in 2 tablespoons of the butter over medium heat just until cooked through, about 2 minutes. Remove from skillet; reserve. If necessary, add remaining 1 tablespoon butter to skillet. Cook onion and garlic until tender, about 2 minutes. Add mushrooms; cook 1 minute. Stir in broth and tomato paste. Return beef to skillet; heat through. Remove from heat. Stir in sour cream. Spoon over each potato.

CHEESE AND PEPPER STEAK STUFFER

Partially freezing the meat facilitates slicing into strips. Substitute other favorite cheeses if you like.

Makes 6 servings

¾ pound boneless sirloin steak, cut ½ inch thick

1–2 large onions, cut into wedges

2 tablespoons olive oil

1 medium green bell pepper, cut into ¼-inch-wide strips

6 baked potatoes

Shredded mozzarella cheese

Cut sirloin into strips about ¼ inch thick and 2 inches in length; reserve. In large skillet, cook onions in oil over medium heat until tender and just beginning to brown, 2–3 minutes. Add green pepper. Continue cooking, stirring occasionally, until crisp-tender, about 1 minute. Remove onion and pepper mixture. Increase heat to medium. Add sirloin strips to skillet (add additional oil if necessary). Cook and stir just until cooked through, about 2 minutes. Return onions and peppers to skillet; heat through. Spoon steak and peppers over each potato. Sprinkle with mozzarella.

ITALIAN SAUSAGE AND PEPPER POTATOES

Italian sausage and crisp-tender peppers in a seasoned tomato sauce bring rave reviews when served over hot potatoes.

Makes 4 servings

½ pound mild Italian sausage

2 teaspoons olive oil

1 medium onion, cut into wedges

1 can (15½ or 16 ounces) whole peeled tomatoes

1 medium red or green bell pepper, cut into ¼-inch strips (about 1 cup) or a combination of red and green peppers.

½ teaspoon dried oregano

⅛ teaspoon dried red pepper flakes (optional)

4 baked potatoes

Grated Parmesan cheese

Carefully cut sausage into ½-inch slices; remove casing. Cook sausage in medium skillet over medium-low heat until browned and cooked through, about 25 minutes. Occasionally stir gently, being careful to keep sausage in ½-inch pieces. Remove from skillet; reserve. Drain fat. Add olive oil to same skillet. Cook onion in oil over medium heat until tender. Add tomatoes, bell pepper, oregano, and red pepper flakes. Return sausage to skillet. Bring to a boil; reduce heat and simmer, uncovered, about 5 minutes to reduce liquid slightly. Spoon sausage and pepper over each potato. Sprinkle with Parmesan cheese.

QUICK SAUSAGE SUPPER STUFFER

When you need dinner in a hurry, try this flavorful sausage stuffer. Complete the meal with a tossed green salad.

Makes 4 servings

½ *cup chicken broth*

1 tablespoon honey

1 tablespoon Dijon-style mustard

¾ *pound fully-cooked smoked sausage, cut diagonally into* ¼-*inch-thick slices*

1 medium green bell pepper, chopped coarse (optional)

4 baked potatoes

In medium saucepan or skillet, combine broth, honey, and mustard. Bring to a boil. Continue boiling to thicken slightly, about 2 minutes. Add sausage and pepper. Reduce heat; simmer to heat through, about 2 minutes. Spoon sausage and sauce over each potato.

DILLED SALMON AND CUCUMBER POTATOES

The cool classic salmon, yogurt, and dill combination is a light and refreshing potato topper.

Makes 4 servings

$\frac{1}{4}$–$\frac{1}{3}$ *cup plain yogurt*

1 tablespoon chopped parsley

1 tablespoon chopped green onion (optional)

1$\frac{1}{2}$ teaspoons finely chopped fresh dill or $\frac{1}{2}$ teaspoon dried dill weed

$\frac{1}{2}$ cup chopped seeded, unpared cucumber

1 can (about 16 ounces) red or pink salmon, drained, flaked, bones removed

4 baked potatoes

Fresh dill

Combine yogurt, parsley, onion, dill, and cucumber; mix well. Add salmon. Toss lightly. Spoon salmon mixture over each potato. Garnish with fresh dill.

Note: Salmon mixture may be refrigerated and served chilled over hot potato.

> "A dish fit for the gods."
>
> **SHAKESPEARE**
> *Julius Caesar*

CRUNCHY TUNA MELT

Favorite tuna salad with a crunch is a new taste sensation stuffed into a potato—with cubes of melting cheddar dispersed throughout.

Makes 4 servings

1 can (6½ ounces) chunk light tuna packed in water, drained and flaked

½ cup chopped celery

¼ cup chopped green onion

¼ cup toasted chopped almonds

2 ounces cheddar cheese, cut into ¼-inch cubes

Mayonnaise or your favorite salad dressing (Thousand Island, Creamy Onion, or Italian)

4 baked potatoes

Combine tuna, celery, onion, almonds, and cheese. Stir in mayonnaise to moisten as desired. Place potatoes in ovenproof baking dish or pan. Spoon tuna mixture over each potato. Cover loosely with foil. Heat in 350°F oven for 8–10 minutes, just until cheese begins to melt; or heat potatoes under broiler just until cheese melts; or place potatoes in microwave-safe dish and cook, uncovered, at 50% power 3–4 minutes or until cheese begins to melt.

CRABMEAT SAUTE

A colorful, savory crabmeat sauté made easily with frozen crabmeat.

Makes 4 servings

½ cup finely chopped mushrooms

¼ cup finely chopped onion

2 tablespoons chopped red bell pepper (optional)

2 tablespoons butter or margarine

1 package (6 ounces) frozen crabmeat, thawed, juices reserved

½ cup dry white wine

2 tablespoons finely chopped parsley

Dash cayenne

2 tablespoons heavy cream (optional)

2 tablespoons dairy sour cream (optional)

4 baked potatoes

½ cup shredded Swiss cheese (optional)

In medium skillet, cook mushrooms, onion, and red pepper in butter over medium-low heat until tender. Stir in crabmeat with juices and wine. Cook until liquid evaporates. Stir in parsley and cayenne. Remove from heat. If desired, stir in cream and/or sour cream. Spoon crabmeat over each potato. Sprinkle with Swiss cheese if desired.

BASIL SHRIMP AND CHICKEN

An easy-to-prepare, light tomato-basil sauce makes this shrimp and chicken combination special.

Makes 4 servings

2 chicken breast halves, skinned and boned, cut into 1-inch squares (about 1 cup)

2 cloves garlic, minced

2 tablespoons butter or margarine

1 medium onion, cut into wedges

1 can (8 ounces) tomato sauce

⅓ cup port wine

¼ cup water

1 teaspoon dried basil

¼ teaspoon salt

¼ teaspoon freshly ground black pepper

⅓ pound medium shrimp, shelled and deveined

4 baked potatoes

Chopped parsley

In medium skillet, cook chicken and garlic in butter over medium-low heat until chicken is tender and lightly browned, about 3 minutes; stir occasionally. Remove chicken; reserve. Add onion to same skillet; cook until tender. Drain excess fat if necessary. Return chicken to skillet. Add tomato sauce, wine, water, basil, salt, and pepper. Bring to a boil. Reduce heat and simmer, covered, 5 minutes. Add shrimp. Simmer, covered, until shrimp are cooked through, 3–5 minutes. Spoon shrimp mixture over each potato. Sprinkle with chopped parsley.

CREAMY CHICKEN AND ARTICHOKE TOPPING

The dish takes only minutes to prepare, but guests will savor every bite. Reserve drained artichoke liquid for marinating other favorite vegetables.

Makes 4 servings

4 chicken breast halves, skinned and boned (about ¾ pound)

Salt and pepper

Paprika

1 jar (6 ounces) marinated artichoke hearts

1 tablespoon butter or margarine

1 cup thinly sliced mushrooms

¼ cup chicken broth

¼ cup heavy cream

3 tablespoons chopped pimiento

Cut chicken into 2-by-½-by-½-inch strips. Season to taste with salt, pepper, and paprika; reserve. Drain artichoke hearts, reserving marinade. Coarsely chop artichoke hearts. In large skillet, over medium-low heat, combine 1 tablespoon reserved marinade and butter. Add chicken; cook and stir until lightly browned and almost cooked through, about 2 minutes. Add mushrooms; continue cooking 1 minute. Add artichokes, broth, and cream. Simmer 2–3 minutes to reduce slightly and allow flavors to blend. Stir in pimiento. Spoon chicken and sauce over each potato.

HOT CHICKEN AND SWISS POTATOES

The secret to this delicious stuffing is heating it just until the cheese begins to melt.

Makes 4 servings

1 cup cooked chicken (cut into bite-size pieces)

2 ounces Swiss cheese, cut into ¼-inch cubes

⅓ cup sliced pitted ripe olives

1 tablespoon diced red bell pepper (optional)

1 tablespoon chopped green onion

⅓ cup mayonnaise

1 teaspoon lemon juice

½ teaspoon dried tarragon (optional)

4 baked potatoes

Combine chicken, cheese, olives, pepper, and onion. Gently stir in mayonnaise, lemon juice, and tarragon. Place potatoes in ovenproof baking dish or pan. Spoon chicken evenly over each potato. Cover loosely with foil. Heat in 350°F oven for 8–10 minutes, just until cheese melts; or heat potatoes under broiler, just until cheese melts; or place potatoes in microwave-safe dish and cook, uncovered, at 50% power 3–4 minutes or until cheese begins to melt.

> *"I wish that every peasant may have a chicken in his pot on Sundays"*
>
> **HENRY IV of France**

CHICKEN A LA KING POTATOES

The old favorite, Chicken à la King, comes alive when stuffed into a potato; try the broccoli variation for a colorful flavor and texture contrast.

Makes 4-6 servings

2 tablespoons butter or margarine

3 tablespoons all-purpose flour

Dash salt

1 cup milk

½ cup chicken broth

1 cup cooked chicken (cut into bite-size pieces)

¾ cup sautéed mushroom slices

2 tablespoons chopped pimiento

4-6 baked potatoes

In medium saucepan, melt butter over medium-low heat. Stir in flour until smooth. Add salt. Slowly stir in milk and broth. Cook and stir until thickened and smooth, increasing heat to medium if necessary. Gently stir in chicken, mushrooms, and pimiento. Spoon chicken mixture over each potato.

VARIATIONS

Peas: Add ½ cup cooked green peas to chicken mixture; heat through. Spoon over potato.

Broccoli: Arrange cooked broccoli flowerets over each potato; spoon chicken mixture over each.

Turkey or ham: Cubes of cooked turkey or ham may be substituted for the chicken.

PORK RAGOUT DIJON

Tender cubes of pork in a delectable rosemary-Dijon sauce make stuffed potatoes for even the most special occasion.

Makes 6 servings

1 pound boneless pork, cut into 1-inch cubes

Salt and pepper

2 tablespoons vegetable oil

1 large onion, cut into wedges

1 tablespoon Dijon-style mustard

1 teaspoon dried rosemary, crushed

¾ cup chicken broth

¾ cup dry white wine

2 medium carrots, cut into ¼-inch-thick diagonal slices

1 cup coarsely chopped mushrooms

3 tablespoons chopped parsley

6 baked potatoes

Season pork to taste with salt and pepper. In large deep skillet or Dutch oven, cook pork in oil over medium-low heat until browned on all sides. (Brown pork in two batches if necessary to avoid overcrowding skillet; add more oil if necessary.) Add onion, mustard, rosemary, broth, and wine. Bring to a boil. Reduce heat and simmer, covered, about 30–45 minutes, or until pork is tender and cooked through. Stir occasionally. (Add additional wine and broth if liquid seems to be cooking away too quickly.) Add carrots and mushrooms. Cook, uncovered, over medium heat about 3 minutes, until carrots are crisp-tender. Stir in parsley. Spoon ragout over each potato.

GARDEN TOPPERS

GARDEN TOPPERS

If you haven't stuffed potatoes with nutritious, colorful, flavorful vegetable combinations, you've missed some great potato meals. Vegetables, prepared in almost any way imaginable, taste great paired with baked potatoes.

From choices like Corn Chowder to elegant Sherried Mushrooms, vegetables really shine when stuffed into a hot baked potato. Simple steamed vegetables, casserole combinations, soups—the possibilities are nearly limitless when you consider the bountiful array of fresh, frozen, and canned vegetables available.

And don't forget leftovers—they make great impromptu meals. With a little imagination, stuffed potatoes transform leftover vegetables into exciting new dishes. For example, reheat cooked vegetables—one or a combination— and add a favorite herb or seasoning. Spoon into a seasoned baked potato. Add a sprinkling of bacon or cheese and perhaps a dollop of yogurt for a super side dish in minutes.

Use the recipes in this chapter as starting points to create a wealth of vegetable stuffings and toppings.

> *"To plow is to pray—to plant is to prophesy, and the harvest answers and fulfills."*
>
> **R. G. INGERSOLL**
> **About Farming in Illinois**

GOLDEN VEGETABLE TOPPER

Simplicity shines in this recipe, but flavor reigns supreme.

Makes 4 servings

2 medium onions, sliced (about 2 cups)
2 tablespoons butter or margarine
1 cup shredded carrot
½ cup dry white wine or chicken broth
½ teaspoon salt
4 baked potatoes

In medium skillet, cook onions in butter over medium heat until tender and beginning to brown. Stir in carrot, wine, and salt. Bring to a boil. Reduce heat and simmer, covered, 15 minutes. Spoon onion mixture over each potato.

SHERRIED MUSHROOMS

Mushrooms with a touch of sherry make this a stuffer to accompany the most elegant meal.

Makes 6 servings

½ pound fresh mushrooms, sliced (about 3 cups)
3 tablespoons butter or margarine
2 tablespoons dry sherry
½ cup dairy sour cream
6 baked potatoes
Chopped chives

In large skillet, cook mushrooms in butter over medium-low heat just until tender. Add sherry. Remove from heat. Immediately stir in sour cream. Spoon mushrooms over each potato. Sprinkle with chopped chives.

CORN CHOWDER POTATOES

ZUCCHINI-TOMATO SAUTE

SESAME CHICKEN
WITH SNOW PEAS

CURRIED CHICKEN

CREAMY AVOCADO DELIGHT

Ready in just minutes, this stuffing provides a unique flavor and texture sensation in every bite!

Makes 4 servings

1 medium avocado, cut into 1-inch chunks

1 tablespoon lemon or lime juice

1 medium tomato, chopped (about ¾ cup)

1 package (3 ounces) cream cheese, cut into ½-inch cubes

3 slices bacon, cooked crisp and crumbled

Dash salt

¼ teaspoon freshly ground black pepper

4 baked potatoes

Combine avocado and lemon juice. Toss lightly to coat avocado with juice. Add tomato, cream cheese, bacon, salt, and pepper. Toss gently to combine. Spoon avocado mixture over each potato.

VARIATION

Add ¼ cup very thinly sliced red onion rings to avocado mixture.

GINGER BROCCOLI AND WALNUT TOPPING

An accompaniment with Oriental flair, this is great with pork, chicken, or your favorite simply prepared meat.

Makes 4 servings

¾ cup chicken broth

1–2 tablespoons soy sauce

2 teaspoons cornstarch

¼ teaspoon ground ginger

¼ cup walnut pieces

2 tablespoons vegetable oil

3 cups broccoli flowerets (about ½ pound)

1 cup sliced fresh mushrooms

4 baked potatoes

Combine broth, soy sauce, cornstarch, and ginger. Stir to mix well; reserve. In large skillet or wok, cook walnuts in 1 tablespoon of the oil over medium-low heat until crisp and just beginning to brown. Remove from skillet; drain well and reserve. Add remaining 1 tablespoon oil to skillet. Add broccoli. Cook and stir over medium heat just until crisp-tender, 2–3 minutes. Add mushrooms; continue cooking and stirring 1 minute or until mushrooms are crisp-tender. Immediately stir cornstarch mixture; add to skillet. Cook and stir until thickened. Spoon over each potato. Sprinkle with walnuts.

CORN CHOWDER POTATOES

A potato bowl holds steaming corn chowder, delicately seasoned with a hint of marjoram.

Makes 4 servings

3 slices bacon

⅓ cup chopped onion

¼ cup coarsely chopped celery

1 tablespoon all-purpose flour

1¼ cups milk

1½ cups cooked whole kernel corn

½ teaspoon salt

½ teaspoon dried marjoram leaves, crumbled

4 baked potatoes

Freshly ground black pepper

In medium skillet, cook bacon until crisp; crumble and reserve. Drain all but 2 tablespoons drippings. Cook onion and celery in reserved drippings over medium heat just until tender. Stir in flour until smooth. Gradually stir in milk until smooth. Cook and stir over medium heat until thickened. Stir in corn, salt, and marjoram. Heat through. Spoon corn chowder into each potato bowl. Garnish with reserved bacon and add pepper to taste.

GERMAN-STYLE POTATO SALAD TOPPER

Authentic flavor, but no-fuss and fast!

Makes 4 servings

3 slices bacon
⅓ cup chopped onion
1½ tablespoons sugar
1½ tablespoons all-purpose flour
½ teaspoon salt
½ teaspoon celery seed
½ cup water
¼ cup white wine vinegar
4 baked potatoes
Chopped parsley
1 hard-cooked egg, cut into quarters

In medium skillet, cook bacon over medium heat until crisp; crumble and reserve. Drain all but 3 tablespoons drippings. Cook onion in reserved drippings over medium-low heat until tender. Combine sugar, flour, salt, and celery seed. Add to onion; stir until smooth. Increase heat to medium. Gradually stir in water and vinegar. Cook and stir until thickened and bubbly. Add bacon. Spoon topping over each potato. Garnish each potato with parsley and an egg quarter.

CREAMY SPINACH TOPPER

Relying on frozen spinach, this creamy, seasoned topper is a cinch to prepare.

Makes 4-6 servings

1 package (10 ounces) frozen chopped spinach

1 cup (8 ounces) dairy sour cream or plain yogurt

¼ cup mayonnaise

¼ cup chopped parsley

1 green onion, chopped fine

1 teaspoon seasoned salt

4-6 baked potatoes

Thaw spinach. Drain very well, pressing out all excess moisture. Combine sour cream, mayonnaise, parsley, onion, and salt; stir to mix well. Stir into spinach. Refrigerate or serve immediately. Spoon spinach over each potato. (If desired, spinach mixture may be heated over low heat before spooning over potato.)

VARIATIONS

Creamy Spinach Parmesan: Stir ¼ cup grated Parmesan cheese into spinach mixture.
Creamy Spinach 'n' Bacon: Add 3 slices bacon, cooked crisp and crumbled, to the spinach mixture.

SWEET AND SOUR SPINACH POTATOES

Tangy wilted spinach with bacon provides a unique flavor and texture for the baked potato.

Makes 4 servings

4 slices bacon

½ pound fresh spinach leaves, torn into bite-size pieces

2 green onions, chopped (optional)

¼ cup cider vinegar

2 tablespoons sugar

2 tablespoons water

¼ teaspoon dry mustard

Dash salt

4 baked potatoes

In medium skillet, cook bacon until crisp. Crumble and add to spinach along with onions. Drain all but 2 tablespoons drippings. Add vinegar, sugar, water, mustard, and salt to drippings. Cook over medium-high heat, stirring to dissolve sugar. When dressing boils, pour over spinach. Toss immediately. Spoon over each potato.

ZUCCHINI-TOMATO SAUTE

Add a taste of summer to your next meal; stuff potatoes with a seasoned zucchini and tomato combination.

Makes 4 servings

2 cloves garlic, minced

1 small onion, cut into rings

2 tablespoons vegetable oil

2 medium zucchini, cut into ¼-inch-thick slices (about 2 cups)

1 small green bell pepper, cut into ¼-inch-thick rings

¼ cup water

2 medium tomatoes, cut into wedges

Salt and pepper

4 baked potatoes

Grated Parmesan cheese

In medium skillet, sauté garlic and onion in oil over medium-low heat until tender but not brown. Add zucchini, green pepper, and water. Continue cooking over medium heat, stirring occasionally, until zucchini is crisp-tender, 3–5 minutes. Add tomatoes; cook just until heated through. Season to taste with salt and pepper. Spoon zucchini-tomato mixture over each potato. Sprinkle with Parmesan cheese.

> *"A little in the morning, nothing at noon, and a light supper doth make to live long."*
>
> **ANONYMOUS**

GARDEN SOUP BOWL

Herbed broth and crisp-tender vegetables are perfect companions for baked potatoes. Serve the topped potato in a bowl to hold the savory broth.

Makes 4 servings

1¾ cups chicken broth

1 medium onion, cut into wedges

¼ teaspoon celery seed

⅛ teaspoon freshly ground black pepper

1 cup sliced green beans (½-inch lengths)

1 medium yellow or zucchini squash, cut into 1-inch chunks (about 1 cup)

1 medium carrot, diced

½ teaspoon dried marjoram leaves, crumbled

¼ teaspoon dried basil

4 baked potatoes

In medium saucepan, combine broth, onion, celery seed, and pepper. Bring to a boil. Reduce heat and simmer, uncovered, about 5 minutes or until onion is soft and tender. Add beans, squash, carrot, marjoram, and basil. Bring to a boil. Reduce heat and simmer, uncovered, about 5 minutes or until vegetables are just crisp-tender. Place each potato in a bowl. Spoon soup over each potato.

> *"Who loves a garden*
> *still his Eden keeps,*
> *Perennial pleasures plants,*
> *and wholesome harvests reaps."*
>
> **AMOS BRONSON ALCOTT**
> ***Tablets: The Garden***

RATATOUILLE POTATOES

A ratatouille made of peak-of-the-summer vegetables comes alive over a baked potato.

Makes 6 servings

1 large onion, cut into wedges

1 clove garlic, minced

2 tablespoons vegetable oil

1 small eggplant (about ½ to ¾ pound), pared and cut into 1-inch cubes

1 medium green bell pepper, cut into 1-inch squares

1 medium zucchini, cut into ½-inch-thick slices

2 medium tomatoes, diced

¼ cup water

1 teaspoon sugar (optional)

½ teaspoon salt

½ teaspoon dried basil

½ teaspoon dried oregano

6 baked potatoes

Grated Parmesan cheese (optional)

In large deep skillet, cook onion and garlic in oil over medium heat until tender. Add eggplant. Continue cooking, stirring occasionally, 3–4 minutes or until eggplant begins to brown. (It may be necessary to add additional oil when cooking eggplant.) Add pepper, zucchini, tomatoes, water, sugar, salt, basil, and oregano. Bring to a boil. Reduce heat and simmer, covered, about 20 minutes or until vegetables are desired doneness. Spoon over potatoes while hot, or serve at room temperature. Sprinkle with Parmesan cheese.

51

VEGETABLE CHILI

Be sure to serve this one in a bowl so as not to miss any of the delicious cumin-flavored broth.

Makes 6 servings

1 medium onion, chopped

2 cloves garlic, minced

1 tablespoon vegetable oil

1 can (15½ or 16 ounces) whole peeled tomatoes

1 can (about 16 ounces) great northern or kidney beans, drained

1 cup beef or chicken broth

2 medium carrots, diced

1 large green bell pepper, chopped coarse

2–3 teaspoons chili powder

1 teaspoon sugar (optional)

1 teaspoon ground cumin

6 baked potatoes

Shredded cheddar cheese (optional)

In large deep skillet, cook onion and garlic in oil over medium heat until tender and onion begins to brown. Stir in tomatoes, beans, broth, carrots, pepper, chili powder, sugar, and cumin. Bring to a boil. Reduce heat and simmer, uncovered, 30 minutes. Place each potato in a bowl. Spoon chili over each potato. Sprinkle with cheese if desired.

Note: If crisper pepper is preferred, add during last 10 minutes of cooking.

BLUE CHEESE AND ASPARAGUS

A simple yet special dish, perfect for luncheon or a light supper. Substitute canned or frozen asparagus spears if fresh asparagus is out of season.

Makes 4 servings

12 asparagus spears, cooked crisp-tender

4 baked potatoes

¼ cup chopped tomato

Blue Cheese Topping (see Chapter 1)

4 slices bacon, cooked crisp and crumbled

Place 3 asparagus spears lengthwise on each potato. Sprinkle 1 tablespoon tomato over each. Spoon Blue Cheese Topping over tomato. Sprinkle with bacon.

Note: If hot cheese topping is desired, run potato with toppings under broiler before garnishing with bacon.

"I stick to asparagus, which still seems to inspire gentle thoughts."

CHARLES LAMB
Essays of Elia: Grace Before Meat

CHAPTER FOUR

INTERNATIONAL TREATS

SESAME CHICKEN
WITH SNOW PEAS

CURRIED CHICKEN

NIÇOISE POTATOES

CHOUCROUTE GARNI

BEEF BURGUNDY POTATOES

VEGETABLES PRIMAVERA

QUICK CHILI POTATOES

SKILLET VEAL PARMESAN

QUICK PIZZA-STYLE TOPPER

TACO TOPPER

INTERNATIONAL TREATS

Oriental, Tex-Mex, and Italian Potatoes? Set aside the tortillas and pastas for a while and try substituting potatoes in your favorite international dishes.

The delicate, smooth taste and texture of a baked potato is a perfect foil for the distinct flavors in many ethnic recipes. Cumin, curry, ginger, oregano, and basil—these specialty seasonings make lively potato stuffers.

From Curried Chicken with traditional condiments to Skillet Veal Parmesan in zesty tomato sauce with melting mozzarella, such foreign favorites stuff potatoes to delight family and guests alike. Once you've tried the marriage of the potato and ethnic specialties, you'll be anxious to try favorites from your own repertoire.

Be sure to serve the potatoes in a bowl or deep plate to catch all of the deliciously flavored sauces that season every bite of these ethnic favorites.

The leading potato growers around the globe are the Soviet Union, Poland, France, Germany, the United States (especially Maine and Idaho), the United Kingdom, and Czechoslovakia.

SESAME CHICKEN WITH SNOW PEAS

Crunchy, colorful vegetables paired with the nutty, one-of-a-kind flavor of sesame makes a sensational potato.

Makes 4 servings

¾ *cup chicken broth*

2–3 tablespoons soy sauce

1 tablespoon dry sherry (optional)

2 teaspoons cornstarch

4 chicken breast halves, skinned and boned, cut into 1-inch squares (about 1 cup)

1 teaspoon minced fresh gingerroot

2 tablespoons vegetable oil

1 medium red or green bell pepper, cut into ¼-inch-thick strips.

3 green onions, cut into 1-inch lengths

2 cloves garlic, minced

6 ounces fresh snow pea pods or 1 package (6 ounces) frozen snow pea pods, thawed and drained

4 baked potatoes

2 teaspoons toasted sesame seeds

Combine broth, soy sauce, sherry, and cornstarch. Stir to mix well; reserve. In large skillet or wok, cook chicken and ginger in oil over medium-high heat until chicken is lightly browned and cooked through, 3–5 minutes. Remove chicken; reserve. Add pepper, onions, and garlic. Cook, stirring constantly, 1 minute. Add pea pods. Continue cooking and stirring 30 seconds or until vegetables are crisp-tender. Return chicken to skillet. Immediately stir cornstarch mixture; add to skillet. Cook and stir until thickened. Spoon chicken mixture over each potato. Sprinkle each with sesame seeds.

CURRIED CHICKEN

½ cup plain yogurt
4 baked potatoes
Chopped green onion
Chopped tomato
Chopped peanuts

Chicken curry with the traditional condiments makes a super stuffer.

Makes 4 servings

4 chicken breast halves, skinned and boned, cut into 1½-inch cubes (about 2 cups)
3 tablespoons butter or margarine
½ cup chopped onion
½ cup finely chopped celery
2 cloves garlic, minced
2–3 teaspoons curry powder
⅛ teaspoon dried red pepper flakes
½ teaspoon salt
1 teaspoon sugar
1 cup chicken broth
1 tablespoon chopped parsley

In medium skillet, cook chicken in butter over medium-low heat until tender and lightly browned, about 5 minutes; stir occasionally. (Brown chicken in two batches if necessary to avoid overcrowding skillet.) Remove chicken; reserve. Add onion, celery, and garlic to same skillet. Cook until onion is tender. Stir in curry powder, red pepper flakes, salt, and sugar. Return chicken to skillet. Add broth. Bring to a boil. Reduce heat and simmer, uncovered, about 10 minutes, to reduce liquid slightly. Stir occasionally. Remove from heat. Stir in parsley and yogurt. Spoon curry over each potato. Garnish as desired with green onion, tomato, and peanuts.

NIÇOISE POTATOES

A variation on a classic. Beautiful to serve and a surprisingly different flavor combination.

Makes 4 servings

1 can (7 ounces) solid-pack white tuna, drained and flaked

1 cup sliced green beans (1-inch lengths), cooked crisp-tender

⅓ cup sliced pitted ripe olives

¼ cup very thinly sliced red onion rings

2 tablespoons chopped Italian parsley

¼ cup vinaigrette-style salad dressing (warm, if desired)

4 baked potatoes

1 hard-cooked egg, cut into quarters

1 small tomato, chopped

Anchovies

Combine tuna, beans, olives, onion rings, and parsley. Toss gently with dressing. Spoon tuna mixture over each potato. Garnish as desired with egg, tomato, and anchovies.

> *"A man seldom thinks with more earnestness of anything than he does of his dinner."*
>
> **SAMUEL JOHNSON**
> *Miscellanies*

NIÇOISE POTATOES

QUICK CHILI POTATOES

CHOUCROUTE GARNI

A quick and easy version of the traditional sauerkraut stew; always a winning flavor combination, but especially good atop a potato.

Makes 4 servings

1 medium onion, sliced

1 clove garlic, minced

1 carrot, shredded

1 tablespoon vegetable oil

2 cups sauerkraut, rinsed and drained

¾ cup dry white wine

¼ pound ham, cut into 1-inch squares

¼ pound kielbasa or smoked sausage, cut into ½-inch-thick slices

4 baked potatoes

1 teaspoon caraway seed

Chopped parsley

In large skillet, cook onion, garlic, and carrot in oil over medium heat until tender and lightly browned. Add sauerkraut, wine, ham, and sausage. Bring to a boil. Reduce heat and simmer, covered, 25 minutes, stirring occasionally. Spoon sauerkraut and meats over each potato. Sprinkle with caraway seed and chopped parsley.

BEEF BURGUNDY POTATOES

Hearty, flavorful beef stew stuffs a potato for a complete meal.

Makes 4 or more servings

2 tablespoons all-purpose flour

Salt and pepper

2 pounds beef chuck, cut into 1½-inch cubes

3 slices bacon

Vegetable oil

1 large onion, chopped

2 cloves garlic, minced

2 medium carrots, chopped coarse

2 tablespoons chopped parsley

1 bay leaf

1 teaspoon ground thyme

2 tablespoons tomato paste

1½ cups burgundy wine

1 cup beef broth

1 cup whole button mushrooms or *halved or quartered larger mushrooms*

4 or more baked potatoes

Chopped parsley

Combine flour and salt and pepper to taste. Sprinkle over beef; reserve. In large deep skillet or Dutch oven, cook bacon until crisp. Remove from skillet; crumble and reserve. Add onion and garlic to drippings. Cook over medium-low heat until tender. Remove from skillet and reserve. Add beef to skillet and brown completely on all sides, adding oil as necessary to prevent sticking. (Brown meat in several batches if necessary to avoid overcrowding skillet.) Return beef, bacon, onion, and garlic to skillet. Add carrots, parsley, bay leaf, thyme, tomato paste, wine, and broth. Bring to a boil. Reduce heat and simmer, covered, about 1½ hours or until beef is tender. Stir occasionally. (Add additional wine and broth if liquid seems to be cooking away too quickly.) Add mushrooms during last 10 minutes of cooking. Remove bay leaf. Spoon beef over each potato. Garnish with chopped parsley.

Note: Recipe makes about 6 cups of beef burgundy. Unused portion may be frozen and reheated for later use.

"An aged Burgundy runs with a beardless Port. I cherish the fancy that Port speaks the sentences of wisdom, Burgundy sings the inspired Ode."

GEORGE MEREDITH
The Egoist

S·P·U·D·S

VEGETABLES PRIMAVERA

2 tablespoons grated Parmesan cheese

4 baked potatoes

Toasted pine nuts

An accompaniment elegant enough for the fanciest meal, yet substantial enough for a meal in itself.

Makes 4 servings

1 small onion, cut into rings

2 cloves garlic, minced

2 tablespoons butter or margarine

¾ cup sliced fresh mushrooms

1 cup broccoli flowerets, cooked crisp-tender

1 medium yellow summer squash, sliced ¼-inch thick (about 1 cup), cooked crisp-tender

½ cup fresh green peas, cooked crisp-tender, or thawed frozen peas

5 cherry tomatoes, halved

⅓ cup heavy cream

In medium saucepan, cook onion and garlic in butter over medium-low heat until tender, not brown. Add mushrooms; cook about 1 minute or until tender. In large bowl, combine onion and mushroom mixture with broccoli, squash, and peas. Stir in cherry tomatoes. Add cream to saucepan. Simmer to reduce and thicken slightly. Remove from heat. Whisk in Parmesan. Pour over vegetables. Stir gently to mix. Spoon vegetables and sauce over each potato. Garnish with pine nuts.

VARIATION

Do not combine sauce and vegetables. Instead, top each potato with combined vegetables. Spoon sauce over each.

QUICK CHILI POTATOES

Hearty chili tastes even better stuffed into a potato bowl. Add all of your favorite toppings for a festive touch.

Makes 4 or more servings

1 pound ground beef

1 medium onion, chopped

1 clove garlic, minced

1 can (15½ or 16 ounces) whole peeled tomatoes

1 can (8 ounces) tomato sauce

1 can (15½ or 16 ounces) kidney beans, drained

1 tablespoon chili powder

4 baked potatoes

Shredded cheddar or Monterey Jack cheese

Dairy sour cream
Chopped green onion

In large skillet, cook beef, onion, and garlic over medium heat until beef is no longer pink. Drain excess fat. Stir in tomatoes, tomato sauce, kidney beans, and chili powder. Bring to a boil. Reduce heat and simmer, uncovered, 1 hour; stir occasionally. Spoon chili over each potato. Top as desired with cheese, sour cream, and green onion. (Recipe makes 1 quart chili. Unused portion may be frozen and reheated for later use.)

VARIATION

Substitute favorite canned or homemade chili, with or without beans, if desired.

SKILLET VEAL PARMESAN

A quick and delicious skillet version of the classic—and a great potato stuffer!

Makes 4 servings

TOMATO SAUCE

1 small red or green bell pepper, chopped

½ cup chopped onion

2 cloves garlic, minced

2 tablespoons vegetable oil

1 can (15½ or 16 ounces) whole peeled tomatoes

2 tablespoons tomato paste

2 tablespoons chopped parsley

1 teaspoon dried basil

½ teaspoon salt (optional)

½ teaspoon sugar (optional)

4 veal cutlets (about 1 pound)

Salt and pepper

Flour

Vegetable oil

1 cup (4 ounces) shredded mozzarella cheese

½ cup grated Parmesan cheese

4 baked potatoes

Prepare Tomato Sauce: In large deep skillet, cook pepper, onion, and garlic in oil over medium heat just until tender. Stir in tomatoes, tomato paste, parsley, basil, salt, and sugar. Bring to a boil. Reduce heat and simmer, uncovered, until thickened, about 20 minutes. You should have about 1½ cups of sauce.

Meanwhile, pound veal to ¼-inch thickness. Cut into 1-inch squares. Season to taste with

64

QUICK PIZZA-STYLE TOPPER

salt and pepper. Sprinkle lightly with flour. In large skillet, cook veal in 2 tablespoons oil over medium heat until lightly browned and cooked through, about 3 minutes. (Brown veal in two batches if necessary to avoid overcrowding skillet; add more oil if necessary.) Drain any excess oil. Return veal to skillet in one layer. Sprinkle evenly with mozzarella. Spread Tomato Sauce evenly over cheese. Sprinkle with Parmesan. Heat, over low heat, just until mozzarella melts and veal is heated through. Spoon over each potato.

Traditional pizza flavors in a potato!

Makes 4 servings

1–1½ cups prepared pizza or spaghetti sauce (homemade or canned), heated

4 baked potatoes

Pepperoni slices

Cooked Italian sausage, crumbled

Shredded mozzarella cheese

Grated Parmesan cheese

Spoon pizza sauce evenly over each potato. Top with pepperoni and/or Italian sausage as desired. Sprinkle with mozzarella and Parmesan. If desired, run under broiler to melt cheese.

TACO TOPPER

The potato replaces the tortilla—deliciously.

Makes 4 servings

1 pound ground beef

1 medium onion, chopped

1–3 tablespoons chopped green chilies

1½ teaspoons chili powder

½–1 teaspoon ground cumin

½ teaspoon salt

1 can (8 ounces) tomato sauce

4 baked potatoes

Shredded lettuce

Chopped tomato

Shredded cheddar cheese

Tortilla chips

Taco sauce

Guacamole

In large skillet, cook beef and onion over medium heat until beef is no longer pink. Stir in chilies, chili powder, cumin, salt, and tomato sauce. Bring to a boil. Reduce heat and simmer, uncovered, about 10 minutes, until thickened. Spoon beef mixture over each potato. Top as desired with lettuce, tomato, cheese, tortilla chips, taco sauce, and guacamole.

CHAPTER FIVE

TWICE AS FAST (AND EASY) STUFFING SUGGESTIONS

TWICE AS FAST (AND EASY) STUFFING SUGGESTIONS

Recipes aren't the only means to a great stuffed potato. Don't overlook the myriad of convenience and prepared products that make delectable, quick, and easy stuffers. Supermarkets are full of deli selections and frozen, canned, and packaged products that make great stuffers. And remember those leftovers! Even the most mundane leftovers take on new meaning when creatively stuffed into a baked potato.

The possibilities are endless. Check the following suggestions, then let your imagination take it from there.

Prepare frozen, canned, and packaged foods according to directions, then spoon over prepared potatoes.

- Chilis
- Stews
- Oriental-style meats, poultry, seafood, and vegetables
- Chicken Divan
- Eggplant Parmesan

- Vegetable soufflés
- Vegetables in cheese and other flavored sauces
- Italian-style main dishes
- Mexican and Tex-Mex dishes
- Clam chowder
- Hearty meat or vegetable soups
- Spaghetti, pizza, and other sauces
- Sandwich sauces and spreads

Try using prepared salad dressings and mixes alone or in combination with other ingredients.

- Blue cheese
- Cucumber and onion
- Italian

"New dishes beget new appetites."

THOMAS FULLER
Gnomologia

S·P·U·D·S

- French
- Thousand Island
- Bacon
- Herb
- Poppy seed

Experiment with any of these easy, convenient toppings—they are ready to spoon over prepared potatoes.

- Imitation and real bacon pieces
- Canned French-fried onions
- Process cheese spreads
- Canned tuna, shrimp, crabmeat, ham, chicken
- Seasoning and spice combinations
- Preshredded cheeses
- Flavored cream cheese
- Dips
- Low-calorie sour cream substitutes
- Reduced-calorie margarine and cheeses
- Flavored cheese products
- A dollop of dairy sour cream topped with caviar

Favorite deli take-outs make great stuffers, too:

- Meat salads
- Vegetable salads
- Marinated vegetables
- Cheese spreads
- Favorite sandwich fillings—consider a Reuben or hot pastrami potato!
- Cream cheese and lox

Learn to make leftovers shine:

- *Pot roast and gravy*—Cut roast into thin strips; heat with gravy. Stir in dairy sour cream. Spoon over potato.
- *Pasta sauces*—Spoon heated sauce over potato; top with shredded mozzarella or Parmesan. Or combine with leftover cooked vegetables; spoon over potato.
- *Roast chicken or turkey*—Make into creamy salad with favorite vegetables and bottled salad dressing or mayonnaise. Or stir into favorite cream

TWICE AS FAST (AND EASY) STUFFING SUGGESTIONS

sauce; add cooked vegetables and spoon over potato.

- *Baked ham*—Chop and sprinkle over potato. Sprinkle with shredded cheddar or Swiss cheese.
- *Cheese*—Tuck cubes of favorite cheese (cream cheese, too) into prepared potato; allow cheese to melt slightly.
- *Cheese sauce*—Heat and spoon over potato. Or add cooked vegetables and/or meats.
- *Scrambled eggs*—Toss with chopped chives, leftover crumbled bacon, or chopped ham. Spoon over potato. Sprinkle with cheese. Run under broiler just to heat. Or toss heated leftover eggs with bits of smoked salmon. Spoon over potato.
- *Hard-cooked eggs*—Prepare favorite creamy egg salad; add bacon or ham. Spoon over potato. Top with freshly grated black pepper.
- *Chili*—Heat and spoon over potato. Top with shredded cheese, chopped green onion, and chopped green pepper.
- *Soups*—From gazpacho to corn chowder, cream or broth-based—just spoon over potato.
- *Stir-fried meats and vegetables*—Heat and spoon over potato.

"Be eating one potato, peeling a second, have a third in your fist, and your eye on a fourth."

Old Irish Proverb

INDEX TO RECIPES

INDEX TO RECIPES

> *"Can we ever have too much of a good thing?"*
>
> **CERVANTES**
> *Don Quixote*